The
Wild
Remedy

Journal

For Cindy

First published in Great Britain in 2023 by
Michael O'Mara Books Limited
9 Lion Yard
Tremadoc Road
London SW4 7NQ

A CIP catalogue record for this book is available from the British Library.

This product is made of material from well-managed, FSC®-certified forests and other controlled sources. The manufacturing processes conform to the environmental regulations of the country of origin.

This book contains advice for guidance only and should not be relied upon as an alternative to professional advice from either your doctor or a registered specialist. You are strongly recommended to consult a doctor if you have any medical or other physical concerns. Neither the publisher nor the author can accept any responsibility for any consequences that may follow if such specialist advice is not sought.

ISBN: 978-1-78929-571-9 in paperback print format

1 2 3 4 5 6 7 8 9 10

Interior and cover photography and illustrations by Emma Mitchell
Cover design by Ana Bjezancevic
Designed and typeset by Ana Bjezancevic
Printed and bound in Lithuania

www.mombooks.com

MIX
Paper from
responsible sources
FSC® C107574

The Wild Remedy

Journal

Finding Wellness in Nature

EMMA MITCHELL

Michael O'Mara Books Limited

Beech

Ivy

Wild
rose

Blackthorn

Hawthorn

Found in the
wood 06.11

Spindle

Introduction

I've suffered from mental illness since I was a young adult and I'm constantly seeking simple behavioural ways to alleviate my anxiety and lift my mood alongside my traditional pharmaceutical and therapeutic treatments. Since the pandemic began, there has been a twenty-five per cent increase in the prevalence of anxiety and depression worldwide, caused by grief, long covid and the effects of long-term stress, uncertainty and the impact on work and income. The research showing that contact with nature improves our mental health is extensive and extremely compelling.

My book, *The Wild Remedy*, was published in 2019. In it I relayed the most recent research into how time spent among trees, plants and wildlife activates nerve cell (neuron) pathways in our brains that shift the levels of chemicals (neurotransmitters) that carry the signals that make up our thoughts. Alongside the science underpinning nature's effect on our minds, I wrote about a whole year I spent walking in local green places far more regularly than I had before, to see whether it lifted my mood and alleviated my anxiety. It was very successful, and for this reason I try to spend time in my garden or local woodland every day.

It's clear that neural pathways were laid down in the brains of our ancestors that responded positively to daily trips to forage for food, medicinal plants and materials for tool-making and shelter-building. It made sense for the brains of those ancient humans to give them a mental reward each time they ventured out to find the food and resources they needed from their local environment. The positive feelings induced every time they went out to find the plants, rocks, mud or wood they needed would have made them strive to feel that way again. This created a positive feedback loop, of going out into the landscape, followed by the mental reward of going out, and this would have had a direct impact on their survival.

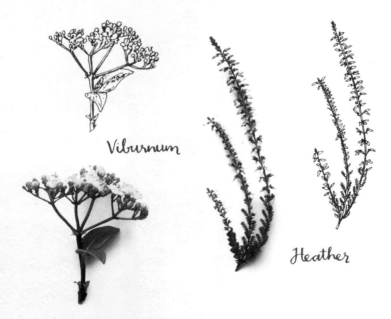

Viburnum

Heather

On average we spend far less time in green places now than we did when these nature-responsive neural pathways were first laid down. It's thought that one reason that mental illness, in particular depression and anxiety, is so prevalent now is that those pathways are no longer being activated to the same level because we spend so much time indoors or in urban environments that are devoid of trees, plants and wildlife.

One way we can improve our mental health consistently is by ensuring we spend time in our garden (if we have one), nearby parks, woodland or countryside as often as possible. Research shows that just fifteen minutes a day among trees and plants has a significant impact on our levels of stress hormone, our heart rate and blood pressure, due to inhalation of plant oils. While we're walking or sitting, we'll also take in visual and auditory information that shift our brain biochemistry even more.

My hope is that using this book you will be able to walk and observe your way through the seasons in your favourite gardens, woodland, park or fields, noticing small changes, recording the behaviour of insects and birds and noting how these simple nature-focused activities alter how you feel. In this way you will trigger the ancient nature-responsive pathways in your brain regularly over the course of the year, and as a result, you will be able to experience how contact with nature really can improve your mental health.

Bank vole

The Brain & 'Flow'

Our thoughts consist of many thousands of small electrochemical signals carried by nerve cells, also called neurons, in the brain. The nerve cells don't touch each other directly to carry the signals forward, instead there are microscopic gaps between them called synapses. The signals are carried across each synapse by chemical messengers called neurotransmitters.

Each neurotransmitter binds its specific receptor molecule in the membrane of the cell that will carry the electrochemical signal onward in the brain. Some neurotransmitters, such as serotonin, dopamine and anandamide, can make the tone of our thoughts more positive, lifting our mood and levels of elation or motivation. One neurotransmitter, called gamma-aminobutynic acid (GABA), is like a set of brakes for our thoughts and when its level increases in our synapses we can feel calmer, and our thoughts will feel less rushed and anxious.

When we're under stress or have had a sudden shock, we release the stress hormone cortisol into our bloodstream. Cortisol is also a neurotransmitter and when its levels increase in our synapses the electrochemical signals that result lead to more rapid, alert thoughts. If there is an excess of cortisol in our bloodstream and brain due to a chronic source of stress, we can feel anxious, and if this continues long-term it can lead to depression.

When we spend time on a creative and/or soothing activity, such as making food from scratch, potting up seedlings or looking carefully for signs of spring in the landscape, our minds can enter a very beneficial mental state known as flow. For this to happen there are a few requirements:

1. Familiarity with the activity (we are proficient at it).

2. We really enjoy the process.

3. There's a repetitive element to the activity, such as chopping ingredients, filling pots with compost or making stitches.

4. We have a strong urge to complete that particular task or project.

If these criteria are met then our brains can enter the flow state, we can lose track of time, feel very relaxed, positive and elated when we complete it. The levels of three neurotransmitters shift when we are in this positive mental state: cortisol levels decrease; dopamine levels increase; anandamide levels increase.

Anandamide is a naturally produced neurotransmitter that is also an endocannabinoid. This means that when it binds its receptor in the brain we experience a natural high. Getting our brains into flow is like taking medically prescribed pharmaceuticals that really do hack our brain, alter its biochemistry significantly and result in a notably lifted mood. We need to try to get ourselves into the flow state as often as we can, and this book can help with that.

Hazel catkins

spring

A New Leaf

Often the very first signs of spring approaching in January or February are subtle changes in foliage in the places you may walk, and in your garden, if you have one. As early as November the leaves of grape hyacinth bulbs (*muscari*) will often be visible above the ground ready for spring and new hawthorn leaves can sometimes emerge in late February or early March.

There is scientific evidence that just looking at plants improves our mental health. For those who may struggle with low mood during the winter months, keeping a close eye on leaf buds in hedgerows or the small green shoots of bulbs is one subtle but reassuring sign that warmer days are round the corner.

Swelling buds of trees and shrubs I spotted

_____

_____

_____

_____

How observing these plant-based seasonal changes made me feel

_____

_____

_____

_____

_____

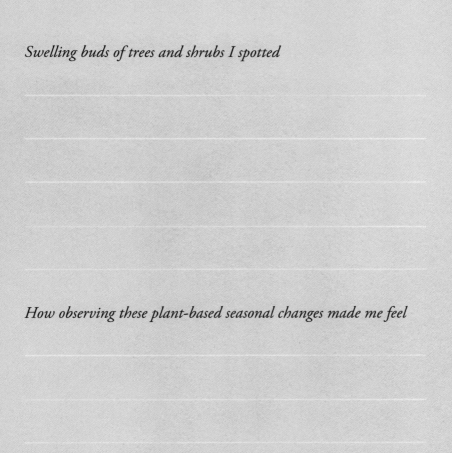

17

First Signs of Spring

Significant nature-based moments in the spring calendar include the arrival of the first swallow, the first blossom (often cherry plum), the first primrose and, for me, the first time I hear the beautiful song of my garden blackbird.

When you witness a significant moment in nature that has meaning or associated memories for you, such as the arrival of a migrant bird, a starling murmuration or a huge drift of poppies, your brain will respond with a significant release of the neurotransmitter dopamine. This will induce intense elation and may even make you feel moved and emotional. These kinds of experiences can have a lasting positive effect on your mental health.

Swallow

Observations and seasonal moments that denote spring for me

_____

_____

Nature-based seasonal signposts I've witnessed this spring (include details, date and site)

_____

_____

_____

How I felt after witnessing these signs (include changes in stress levels or mood)

_____

_____

_____

_____

Nesting Time

Recent research has shown that interactions with birds can improve mental health. Making even small changes to increase your chances of seeing birds in your garden, if you have one, can make a difference to your mood and anxiety levels. Putting out suet seeds and mealworms can benefit both you and any feathered visitors. In spring, birds need all the extra energy they can get.

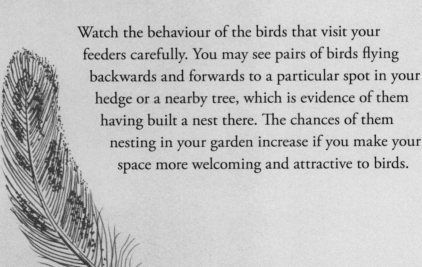

Watch the behaviour of the birds that visit your feeders carefully. You may see pairs of birds flying backwards and forwards to a particular spot in your hedge or a nearby tree, which is evidence of them having built a nest there. The chances of them nesting in your garden increase if you make your space more welcoming and attractive to birds.

*Bird species I've seen
this spring*

_____

_____

_____

Evidence for nests I've seen locally

_____

_____

_____

Birds I'm hoping to see on future walks

_____

_____

_____

seedlings

Things can often feel bleak in the early weeks of spring, especially if sunshine is scarce. Simply choosing from beautiful seed catalogues is likely to trigger the release of dopamine. Spending just ten or fifteen minutes sowing flowers for summer is likely to put your mind into the flow state. This will alleviate anxiety and lift your mood.

Keep your seed trays moist and create a small ritual of scanning the surface of the compost each morning for the first signs of tiny green shoots. The sight of your first seedlings will trigger the release of yet more dopamine and this will continue as your seedlings grow and flower.

Cow parsley
Anthriscus sylvestris

Wildflowers and hardy annuals I'd love to grow this year.
The species I've sown

_____

_____

_____

How the sight of my first seedling shoots has made me feel

_____

_____

_____

My plans with these new flowering plants in the seasons to come

_____

_____

_____

Mycobacterium Vaccae

When we interact with soil or compost, we come into contact with *Mycobacterium vaccae*, a benign bacterium. This microbe stimulates our brains to release the positive neurotransmitter serotonin. This mucky practice can be quite meditative at times.

Create an opportunity to sink your hands into soil. This could be planting your flower seeds, weeding or potting indoors. It's an opportunity to feel the soft, moist, cool earth against your hands.

1. Find a comfortable spot, whether you are planting or weeding. Gently close your eyes.

2. Breathe in deeply. Be aware of any thoughts you are having. When your mind wanders, focus on your breath and the sensations in your hands.

3. Focus on the sense you detect, the feeling of the compost or the scent of the plants nearby. Inhale deeply.

4. Gently open your eyes when you are ready.

How I felt before

_____

_____

How I feel afterwards

_____

_____

If you're feeling low, immerse yourself in the botanical details in my photo.

Searching for Colour

The landscape in the early weeks of spring can often be persistently dingy, brown, even bleak. Any hint of brightness and colour can be so welcome, even if it's a tiny forget-me-not or the glimpse of a robin's reddish breast. This is the time of year when I often search avidly for floral colour in the garden or local hedgerows. It can be found, but its scarcity makes it especially precious.

When humans see something they think is beautiful, dopamine is released, leading to lifted mood, and certain colours such as pinks and blues have been shown to bring calm to the viewer. For these reasons it really is worth scouring your patch for colour to photograph or bring indoors on dark early spring days.

Primrose

Sources of spring colour I've noticed

How discovering spring colour has changed the way I feel

Springtime Flow

Spending time in a green space, be it a garden, woodland or coastal path, slowing down or sitting a while in order to notice details you may miss can induce a very beneficial state in our brains. The flow state is induced in the brain when we're on semi-autopilot and really enjoying a particular activity. Crafts, gardening and exercise can induce flow, but I also find it happens when I'm closely observing very small details of plants and animals while on walks.

Simply making the decision to seek out the distinctive leaf shapes of certain plants or collecting shells or patterned feathers along the shore can put your mind into the flow state. Directing your mind towards the flow state can lower anxiety and lift mood significantly and this can benefit mental health in a lasting way if you consistently pursue activities that switch your mind into that mode.

Signs of spring I found while walking

_____

_____

_____

Changes in how I felt afterwards

_____

_____

_____

Long-lasting changes I notice from my spring walks

_____

_____

_____

Wild
marjoram

Bluebells & Orchids

Bluebells (*Hyacinthoides non-scripta*), also known as 'fairy flowers' or 'wood bells', are one of the most beautiful flowers of spring. Flowering from March to May, their deep, intense blue hue is mesmerizing when they grow in dense drifts forming a carpet on woodland floors or along rural roads. I often sit and gaze at them, absorbing their vibrant colour and floral scent. Undisturbed woodland is the perfect place to find them, along with roadside verges and parks.

In April, early purple orchids will appear, often in the same undisturbed ancient woodland as bluebells. Pyramidal orchids (*Anacamptis pyramidalis*) favour chalky soils and flower right at the end of spring and into early summer. There's a place of special scientific interest near where I Iive and one spring, in a sight that was almost unreal, I came across literally hundreds of flowering pyramidal orchids.

How the vastness of bluebells in spring makes me feel

_____

_____

_____

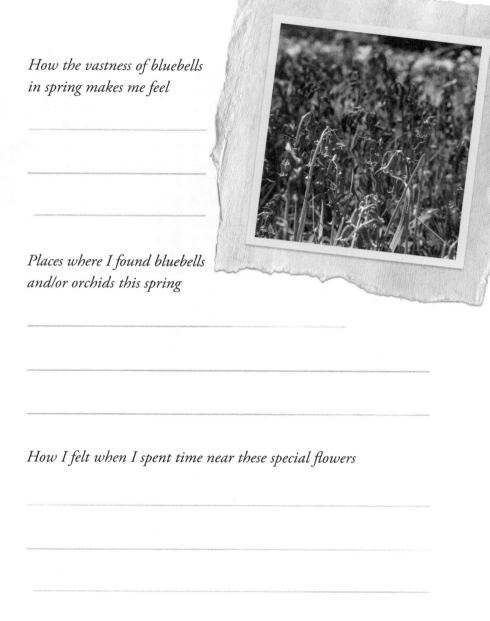

Places where I found bluebells and/or orchids this spring

_____

_____

_____

How I felt when I spent time near these special flowers

_____

_____

_____

scents of spring

When humans inhale the oils released by plants (phytoncides) there are a range of positive effects in our bodies, and the significant decrease in our stress hormone levels that ensues can result in us feeling less anxious. Seeking out particular botanical scents in your garden or on spring walks will result in improved mental health that can last for hours.

Examples of scented plants to seek out include wild garlic, wild marjoram, bluebells and the leaves of yarrow. The olfactory centre of the brain is very close to the hippocampus, which stores and controls memory, which is why scents can often evoke emotional memories. For me, the intense mix of phytoncides that creates the scent of mown grass reminds me of my grandad's garden when I was small.

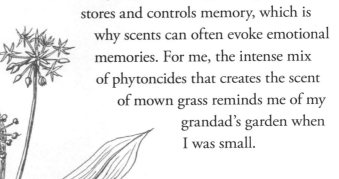

Wild garlic

Wild scented species I've encountered and identified this season

_____

_____

_____

_____

_____

Botanical scents that evoke memories for me

_____

_____

_____

_____

_____

_____

Cow parsley
Anthriscus sylvestris

Cow Parsley

Cow parsley (*Anthriscus sylvestris*) is my favourite plant. Known as 'Mother die', 'Wild chervil' and 'Keck', in spring its frothy flowers line the hedgerows and verges. This beautifully lacy wildflower represents high spring for me. Its seedlings can be seen from the previous August and it flowers in May and June.

1. Look at the uppermost cow parsley stem in my illustration opposite, that's pointing slightly to the right.

2. Focus on and draw the main stem and then the small stemlets emerging from the top.

3. Add the tiny florets at the top of the stemlets by adding five very small oval shapes to each. Continue the main stem down and add the small leaflets and immature flowers either side.

Seasonal Check-in

Places I've walked since spring began

Spring observations that had the most meaning for me

Familiar species I've seen while walking

Species I've seen that were new to me

_____

_____

*Ways in which I've helped to rewild and increase the biodiversity
in my area this season*

_____

_____

_____

_____

Blackthorn blooms

Summer

Bee Friendly

Bees are a quintessential part of a summer garden, meadow, verge or hedgerow and their pollinator role in our food production is crucial, but several aspects of large-scale farming are posing a significant threat to bee survival around the world.

The use of pesticides has been linked to the decline of bee numbers. Neonicotinoid pesticides have halved honeybee populations over the past twenty-five years. In Denmark, farmers are encouraged to plant five per cent bee-friendly flowers, encouraging biodiversity. We can do the same, creating an environment that invites bees to thrive.

Providing a range of bee-friendly wildflowers along with a bee hotel will really help your local bees to thrive. Make your own with pieces of hollow bamboo, or hollow plant stems, bundled together.

1. Using an untreated wooden plank, make a rectangular frame around 15–20cm x 10–15cm (6–8 inches x 4–6 inches).

2. Drill holes for the screws, to stop the wood from splitting, and assemble the frame.

3. You will need plenty of hollow stems of different diameters. To attract a wide array of bees, make sure the width of your holes range from 2.5–10mm (0.1–0.4 inches). You can use hogweed, bamboo or reed stems.

4. Cut them to 10cm (4 inches, or the depth of the wood you used) and carefully pack them into your frame.

5. Add a backing board and then attach your bee hotel to a south- or south-east-facing wall or fence.

Pollinator Watch

Focusing your attention on bees, hoverflies and other pollinators of flowers in your garden or on walks is likely to shift your mind into the flow state, alleviating anxiety and conferring a gentle, natural high. Make notes of the patterns and colours of stripes on the bees you see and use a bee identification chart to find out which species these are. If you can also identify the flowers they're visiting then you're beginning to learn about bee–plant relationships.

Painted lady

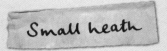
Small heath

Descriptions of the pollinators I noticed

Bee species I identified while watching

Confirmed bee–plant interactions I spotted

Ground Connection

Whether it's through gardening, planting, weeding or simply sitting on a lawn, a wild patch of grass or the floor of a woodland, connecting directly with the ground is a soothing mind hack when you need it most.

Sniff the soil or compost – this sounds strange but it will increase the chances of you coming into contact with beneficial bacteria. Think of it in the same way as the ingestion of beneficial bacteria for your gut, but in this case it's for your brain and mental health.

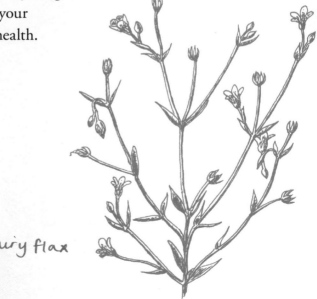

Fairy flax

My favourite spots to connect with the earth

_____

_____

How I felt before

_____

_____

Where I was and what I saw while I was there

_____

_____

How I felt after connecting with the ground

_____

_____

Ladybird

Ladybirds (or ladybugs as they're known in the US) are recognizable by their bright red-orange wing covers and familiar oval shape. They belong to the *Coccinellidae* family of beetles and are sometimes named after the number of their spots. They make excellent drawing subjects. You can draw them all year round but if you're a beginner, it may be worth waiting until winter when they hibernate (see photograph opposite). Creating art has been shown to dial down the stress hormone cortisol. For this you'll need paper, a pen, coloured pencils and/or paints.

1. Begin by drawing an oval shape for the body.

2. Draw a small half oval for the head. Create a line down the centre of the oval.

3. Add the spots, ensuring you place a central spot just behind the head.

4. Add six legs and two antennae.

5. Add colour with paint, pencils or pens.

Rockpooling

Since I was small, the creatures that inhabit rockpools have fascinated me. The strange beings that live in these tiny worlds with their harsh conditions sparked my urge to become a naturalist.

Gazing into a tidal pool to spot crabs, shrimps and sea anemones and watching the interactions between these species can grab your attention completely, especially if you capture a few inhabitants and watch them for a while in a temporary rockpool you've made in a bucket. Regressing to childhood pleasures can lift mood significantly and this is a wonder-filled way to do so.

Common periwinkle

Species I identified in rockpools

How I felt before and after rockpooling

Species I'd still like to encounter in a rockpool

Acorn barnacle

This page is for your drawings.

Flower Press

Seeking out and picking flowers from your garden or common ones found on a walk will shift your neurotransmitter balance for the better. Pressing flowers creates a precious resource, as simply looking at the summery botanical moment you'll have captured will lift your mood during winter.

Common flax

Common Knapweed

Field Scabious

You'll need at least two pieces of kitchen towel or blotting paper and a heavy weight: a pile of books will work well.

1. Gather a small bunch of flowers from your garden or on your walk. (Note: only collect one wildflower specimen of each species and only if it's very common.)

2. Pat them dry to prevent them becoming mouldy while being pressed.

3. Place a piece of kitchen towel or blotting paper towards the back of a book and arrange your flowers on it.

4. Place another piece of kitchen towel/blotting paper on top of the first piece, close the book and put more heavy books on top.

5. Wait for the flowers to press and dry. The drying time will depend on the thickness of your flowers and can take up to four weeks.

seashells

Looking at the fractal patterns in nature (see page 119), such as those made by tree branches or the veins on the back of a leaf, has been shown to increase the speed of recovery from stress by sixty per cent. This hints at the existence of an ancient neural pathway in our brains that's connected with foraging. The fractal spiral patterns of shells can decrease stress levels and collecting a few while visiting the shore will confer the extra benefit of dopamine release triggered by finding something you're looking for.

If you arrange your shells carefully to create a gentle gradation of colour, this process is likely to put your mind into flow and lift your mood. Photograph the arrangement you've made and leave it on display so that your brain will benefit from seeing it whenever you pass by. Note: don't collect many shells, just a very few of the most common type.

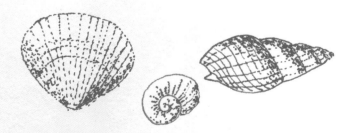

The beach I visited and the species
of shell I found

_____

_____

The full range of colours I see while looking at the shells closely

_____

_____

How I felt before and after arranging the shells

_____

_____

The types of shells I would love to find

_____

_____

Summer Birdsong

Most birdsong comes to an end in July as the majority of species will have raised at least one brood by then and the males will begin to conserve the energy needed to proclaim their territories. Savouring the dawn and evening choruses throughout June can improve your mental health.

Research shows that listening to birdsong can be as effective as meditation apps at alleviating anxiety, and when we learn something new, such as individual birds' songs and calls, dopamine is released, increasing motivation and lifting mood.

Goldcrest

My favourite bird species and why

_____

_____

_____

Species I've identified by recognizing their calls

_____

_____

_____

How learning about these bird species has made me feel

_____

_____

_____

_____

The patterns found in
nature calm our minds.
Look carefully at this
page if you're feeling
strung out.

_____

_____

_____

_____

_____

_____

Summer Night Walk

When the days are uncomfortably hot, seeking out and recording nocturnal wildlife can be the antidote. Walking at night provides an opportunity to witness a plethora of shy wildlife that you miss during daylight hours.

Summer ushers in the possibility of encountering moths, owls, badgers and hedgehogs, even in urban areas. Arrange a night-time walk with a friend; the social interaction you'll experience with them will induce oxytocin release in both of you: a positive neurotransmitter responsible for feelings of connection and safety.

You'll need a torch. As you walk, listen out for owl calls and watch carefully for glimpses of larger mammals such as rabbits, foxes and deer, and take note of sounds of chirps and fluttering. Look up and you might be lucky enough to see bats flitting across the night sky.

Species I hope to see while night-walking

_____

_____

Species I encountered while night-walking

_____

_____

How the night-time wildlife encounters made me feel

_____

_____

Seasonal Check-in

Places I've walked since summer began

_____

_____

Nature-based highlights for me

_____

_____

Encounters with wildlife that altered my mood

_____

_____

_____

_____

New species I've seen and/or recorded this summer

_____

_____

_____

_____

Species I really hope to spot during summers to come

_____

_____

_____

_____

_____

Bee Orchid

Red campion

Common knapweed

Cow parsley

Nipplewort

Autumn

Wild carrot

Breadseed poppy

Feverfew

Harvest

Autumn is traditionally a time of harvest in ancient calendars and connecting, even in a small way, with this kind of activity can help to forge a deeper relationship with your local nature spots, particularly as the season shifts, and will result in a dopamine release as you forage for wild fruit.

If you walk in green spaces near your home, watch out for ripening berries, rosehips, haws (the berries of the hawthorn) and wild apples. Find new routes for your walks and take a bag or box with you to collect your finds. If you enjoy a liqueur, infuse haws and rosehips in gin (see recipe in my book *Making Winter*), and combine blackberries and any wild apples you may find in your baking. Freezing some of your small but precious harvest will give you a welcome lift during winter.

Blackberries

On my walk, I collected

With my harvest, I made

On my harvest walk, I felt

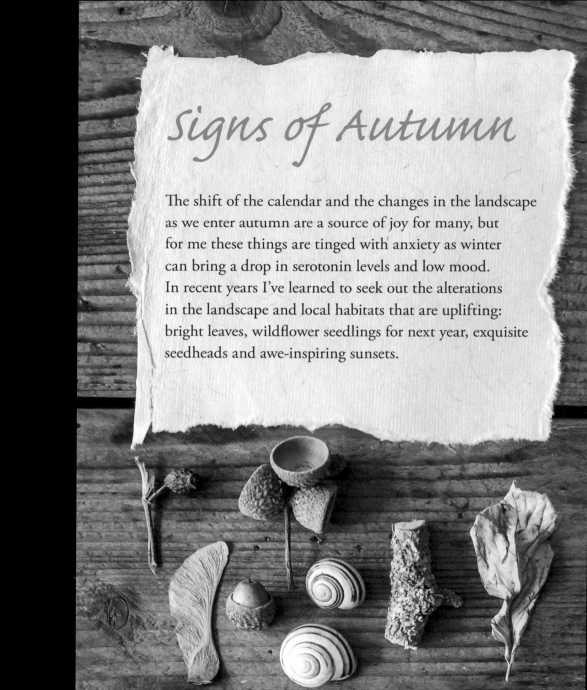

Signs of Autumn

The shift of the calendar and the changes in the landscape
as we enter autumn are a source of joy for many, but
for me these things are tinged with anxiety as winter
can bring a drop in serotonin levels and low mood.
In recent years I've learned to seek out the alterations
in the landscape and local habitats that are uplifting:
bright leaves, wildflower seedlings for next year, exquisite
seedheads and awe-inspiring sunsets.

The changes that I noticed in my area

_____

_____

_____

_____

The local botany I noticed emerging or receding

_____

_____

_____

The shift in mood during these autumn months is

_____

_____

_____

Migrant Birds

As the breeding season ends and autumn begins, some bird species that epitomize summer, such as swallows and swifts, leave for their winter feeding grounds. I find this thought can make me regret the onset of autumn but to counter this, several species of water birds and the migrant thrushes arrive in the coming weeks. Spotting a skein of geese flying over a hedgerow or a mixed flock of redwings and fieldfares feasting on haws on a crisp day can compensate for the lack of swallows in the sky. Visiting the coast or wetlands with a pair of binoculars may reward you with the sight of migrant birds and lift your mood.

Redwings

Migrant bird species I have spotted (include details, date and site)

_____

_____

_____

Migrant bird species I would still like to see

_____

_____

_____

How spotting these feathered travellers has made me feel

_____

_____

_____

_____

Self heal

Borage

Chicory

Field scabious

Red campion

Wild marjoram

Red clover

Wild carrot

Yarrow

Lady's
bedstraw

Ox eye
daisy

Field
poppy

Looking at the small botanical details here can alleviate anxiety.

Sensory Walk

As the sun moves further away from the northern hemisphere, the colour of the light shifts to become golden. The leaves will change colour as the chlorophyll is withdrawn from them and the reds of polyphenols and the yellows and oranges of carotenoids are exposed. There's always a shift in the scents that can be detected in green spaces – it smells more earthy and delicious, like the very best compost.

Research has shown that carefully noticing these kinds of external sensory experiences increases positive emotions in people with residual depression. Dedicating just fifteen minutes two or three times a week to connecting to the autumnal landscape and the autumnal changes in this way can help prevent the seasonal low mood that can descend during winter.

The textures I can feel

_____

_____

The sounds I can hear

_____

_____

The autumnal colours I can see

_____

_____

How autumnal sensory experiences make me feel

_____

_____

Dried Botanical Finds

I found by accident that after drawing plant specimens or picking them and not using them in photographs, I would sometimes leave them on a tabletop for a day or two. They dried readily and became desiccated without any effort from me.

These dried stems, flowers and leaves have a faded and delicate frailty, and you can preserve any garden or common wildflowers you come across during the autumn to create very long-lasting displays and posies.

Ivy

Spindle

1. Look out for late flowers in your garden or on your walks. Perfect autumnal flowers to collect a few specimens of include yarrow, especially if it's slightly pink, and toadflax.

2. Lay the flowers out on kitchen towel or blotting paper on a tabletop or other surface. Avoid doing this in a kitchen or bathroom as the air is usually quite moist, the drying won't happen efficiently and there's a chance your flowers might become mouldy.

3. Use your dried flowers in a permanent arrangement in a vase or jar, or keep one or two nearby while you work, to lift your mood.

Wild rose

Blackthorn

Leaf Watch

In the months following summer, the seedlings of wildflowers that will have germinated during the summer will capitalize on the warmest days and develop leaves and roots. The leaves of annual flowers such as cow parsley, wild carrot and even cleavers/sticky weed are signs of spring, which is a really heartening thought. Focusing on small new leaves on your walks as they develop and grow will give you a lift throughout the coming winter.

1.   Try to remember where you may have seen your favourite wildflowers in bloom during the spring and summer.

2.   In those spots, search carefully for the remains of the plants and for smallish new leaves nearby.

3.   Look very closely at the leaves and compare them to images online or in plant-identification apps of the leaves of the wildflowers you saw earlier in the year.

4.   If there's a match, continue to visit these seedlings through the autumn and winter.

5.   If there isn't a match, watch the seedlings anyway and record the fully grown plants that result when spring arrives.

Beautiful Seedheads

I think that seedheads can be as beautiful as flowers. Of course they lack colour, but they're often far longer-lasting than petals and stamens and have gorgeous tiny chalice- or lacy-cage-like shapes that can last well into the following year. Watch out for flowers that have faded and been replaced by their seedheads. Particularly beautiful are those of red campion, wild carrot and cowslips. If you gather some to bring home, make sure you scatter any seed where they were growing first.

Seedheads I've learned to identify this autumn

_____

_____

Seedheads I've gathered to bring home

_____

_____

Collecting Autumn Colours

The range of colours that can be seen in autumn can be astonishing. Some of these common spindle leaves (*Euonymus europaeus*) pictured are the brightest pink. Seeking sources of autumnal colour, bringing them home and arranging them carefully with gentle gradations of colour will significantly increase the amount of dopamine and natural cannabinoid released into your synapses and improve your mood.

Call of the Owl

As a child I lived in Liverpool and I remember hearing tawny owls call occasionally and the intense wonder I felt at that auditory window onto a wild nocturnal world, even in an urban setting. One night in autumn I saw a tawny owl on a nearby house and I was enchanted by seeing this secretive bird.

Walking in a tree-rich green space on autumn nights might bring you the same positive shift in thought. Listening out for and then hearing owl calls is likely to induce awe, which will increase parasympathetic arousal and decrease ruminating thoughts.

On my owl-watch I noticed (include details, date and site)

The species of owl I heard and/or saw

The way the owl's call made me feel

Tawny owl

Sunset

There's strong evidence that our mental health improves if we experience awe: that feeling of wonder induced by witnessing something overwhelmingly beautiful. When summer ends, sunsets can often be humblingly lovely, full of rich, almost unearthly colours and made into a living artwork when viewed in front of statuesque seedheads. Witnessing the shifting pinks, oranges and purples as the light alters is very likely to induce intense dopamine release conferring lasting elation.

Sunsets I witnessed (include details, date and site)

_____

_____

How I felt afterwards

_____

_____

song of the Wren

The wren is one of the only birds that continues to sing into autumn. Researchers at King's College, London, found that encounters with birds improve mental health and that birdsong reduces anxiety. Male wrens won't sing every day outside the breeding season but listen carefully to any birdsong you hear near your home or in the places you may walk regularly. Every wren's song contains a trill and recognizing those gorgeous notes will lift your mood as well as bringing calm as the days grow colder.

Wren

1. The place and time I heard birdsong during autumn.

2. Listening carefully, did that song contain a trill?

3. If so, it's a wren; were you able to see it? Binoculars may help.

4. Keep returning to or near that spot. Have you heard or seen the wren again? Have you identified a wren's song elsewhere?

Seasonal Check-in

New species I've noticed and recorded this autumn

Walks and/or encounters that lifted my mood

Small, beautiful details I noticed

Sloes on
blackthorn

*Species I'd like to see or attract to my garden
in the season to come*

Barn owl

Tawny owl

Little owl

Winter

Kestrel

Great spotted woodpecker

Pheasant

Winter Intentions

It's at this point in the year that I begin to remind myself of all the things I can do to keep the detrimental effects of low light levels at bay. Seasonal affective disorder (SAD) is a temporary but potentially debilitating depression that can descend in winter as a result of our exposure to fewer hours of sunlight. A thickly clouded sky and dingy weather can make venturing out on a walk feel almost impossible at times. The nature spotter's high that can help to sustain my mental health seems ever more elusive. There are nature-based mind hacks and simple strategies that research shows can and will help, which I try to adopt in winter.

Hawthorn

Small seasonal routines to keep myself mentally well this winter

_____

_____

_____

_____

Activities I've tried in previous winters that have been effective

_____

_____

_____

_____

_____

Seasonal Creativity

Choose a creative, preferably nature-inspired project to work on during the colder months: something that can be made slowly over several weeks or even months. For example, you could try drawing plant specimens that you might regularly find on walks or in your garden, to create a winter botanical journal. This sort of daily creative ritual will increase your chances of shifting your brain into the flow state on a regular basis.

There are some requirements that increase the likelihood that your brain will enter this state: familiarity with the creative process, an urge to complete that project and something that you love doing. If these criteria are met and your mind enters flow, then your stress hormone (cortisol) levels will decrease, your dopamine levels will increase and you'll release anandamide, the bliss chemical in your brain, inducing a natural high.

For really difficult days that might arise in winter, making a cosy nest to which you can retreat to work on your project will help your mental health further (see Emergency Override on page 112).

Virtual Nature

There are days when getting out into green spaces may not be possible, especially with the arrival of much wetter weather. On days when you want to simply stay warm and dry indoors, your mental health can still benefit from nature. Researchers from the National Park Service and Colorado State University found that listening to pleasant natural sounds can reduce cortisol and lower blood pressure, so when you're unable to make it outdoors, seek out the sounds of nature via the internet.

The Radio Lento podcast has beautiful sound 'postcards'. These simple, charming sounds will activate the auditory neural pathways that respond to being among trees and plants and will help you through the colder months.

Goldcrest

My favourite sounds in nature and how they make me feel

_____

_____

_____

Online sources I've used without having to venture outside

_____

_____

_____

Ways in which these virtual, nature-based sources have helped me

_____

_____

_____

*The details on this page
will calm your thoughts,
so take a moment to
look closely.*

Fossil Hunting

Fossil hunting at Folkestone, Walton-on-the-Naze or the Deep History coast of Norfolk is one of the activities that brings me the most relief if my mood is low and I'm mentally exhausted. After a storm, fossilized sea urchins, sharks' teeth and belemnites are easier to find as the action of the waves scours them from soft sediments.

Seeking out these ancient stone treasures is just one of the nature-based activities that can trigger a surge of dopamine in the brain. It's released when we find the elusive pattern of an echinoid or the beautiful arc of ammonite.

Pyritized twigs from the 56-49m. year old London Clay layer. During this era Britain's climate was subtropical.

Striatolamia sharks' teeth from the London Clay. 50 million years ago sharks & turtles swam off the Essex coast.

1.   For a fossil-hunting trip you'll need warm and waterproof clothing and shoes and a plastic bag for your specimens.

2.   Look online for the best fossil-rich places near you (www.ukfossils.co.uk is fantastic for this).

3.   At the beach/fossil-rich site, keep your eyes peeled for small ridged or spotty patterns on the pebbles and rocks you see.

4.   Once home, identify your fossils by searching the internet for images of similar specimens found at the site you visited.

5.   Make a display of what you find by carefully laying them out and labelling them like a small museum exhibit.

Winter Flowering

One simple way we can alleviate the negative toll winter can take on our minds is with winter-flowering plants. Even the smallest outdoor space can improve your mental health between November and March if you plant it with heathers, early flowering hellebores, pink snowberry and primroses. If you have enough space, plant a winter-flowering cherry tree.

Watching the progress of the buds and flowers of these precious species can provide a sort of botanical stepping stone to spring. Having a few of these beautiful flowers and berries nearby will induce lots of small dopamine bursts over the course of the season.

Snowberry

Hellebore

How wintry landscapes can make me feel

*My favourite winter-flowering garden plants (including those
I've planted in my garden)*

Ways in which seeing these plants has made me feel

The Solace of Birds

The research showing that interactions with birds can improve human mental health can be used to such good effect during the winter months. If you hang out a range of food for the birds somewhere where you can watch them easily – sunflower seeds, peanuts, dried mealworms and fat-rich bird snacks – you'll be rewarded with daily visitors that will lift your mood and bring calm while you watch them. As you increase the birds' chances of surviving through till spring, your mental health will feel the benefit too.

House sparrow

My favourite garden birds

Garden birds I have fed in previous winters

How seeing birds through my window makes me feel

The changes I notice in my day-to-day mood after sightings

Winter Collections

I make collections of small finds through the year
but the gently thrilling process of finding a perfect
feather, pine cone or cluster of berries can make
the biggest difference to mental health in winter.
Discovering each small treasure will induce the
release of dopamine, and arranging them with gentle
gradations of colour once I get home is likely to help
my mind relax into the flow state.

Emergency Override

Many people have lower energy in the winter. A key reason for this is fewer sunlight hours leading to lower levels of serotonin, along with unpleasant weather making walks impossible.

On the most difficult days the best route to self-compassion is to embrace the urge to hibernate. Snuggling under a blanket activates neural pathways triggered when we cuddle another human or pet. Inhaling plant oils from a scented candle containing them or simply some fresh herbs or dried lavender while nestled under some cosy textiles will dial down your cortisol and calm you even further.

Muntjac deer

For some emergency dopamine see my photographic collections within each season.

How I feel on the most difficult days of winter

Reasons for this stress and/or low mood that I can identify

Emergency strategies that help me through tough times

This page is for your drawings.

solstice

If you struggle with low energy and mood in winter, there's a threshold in late December that may help. The winter solstice usually falls on 21 December and is the day of least sunlight, but every day afterwards we begin to gain more minutes of light as the sun moves towards the northern hemisphere once more. To help you through the lead-up to these weeks with the lowest light levels, try to sit or walk outside in the winter sun whenever you feel able, to increase your serotonin levels and to look for even the tiniest signs of the new season approaching.

How I feel on the most difficult days of winter

_____

_____

_____

How reaching the solstice can make me feel

_____

_____

_____

Why my feelings change after midwinter

_____

_____

_____

Fractals

Fractals are patterns that repeat themselves on several scales in the same structure and they are common in nature. Seeking these beautiful patterns on difficult winter days can be an effective mind hack. Examples of fractals in nature that you could seek out include the patterns of the branches of a tree, looking for ferns and collecting pine cones and empty shells. Our ancestors were closely connected with the natural world and it's likely that their brains evolved to respond to fractals. Those pathways are still in place and can help alleviate seasonal stress in modern humans.

Fractals I have spotted from my local area (include the details)

The First Blossom

One of the things I become almost obsessed with as January comes to an end is seeking out the first botanical signs of spring approaching in the local countryside. I loiter near cherry plum trees because this tree opens its spring blossom first. I'll stare at primrose buds, willing them to open, and I'll walk for miles in driving sleet to visit nearby goat willow or pussy willow.

Searching for the first signs of the new season to come will not only confer the benefits of a walk among trees and plants – a decrease in cortisol, blood pressure and heart rate – but also the heady feeling of relief, caused by dopamine release at seeing small but tangible signs that warmer and sunnier days are ahead.

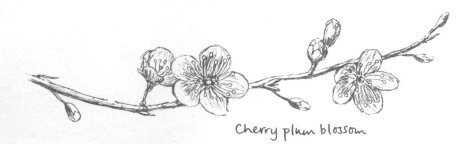

Cherry plum blossom

My favourite signs of spring, botanical or otherwise

_____

_____

_____

Signs of spring I intend to seek out

_____

_____

_____

Signs of spring I have encountered (include the details, date and site and how they made me feel)

_____

_____

_____

Seasonal Rhythms

Establishing routines and small daily rituals can offer reassurance to a mind struggling with seasonal gloom. It may be difficult to muster the motivation for a full-blown walk, but getting outside to sit for a short while is more manageable.

There is evidence that exposing your eyes to sunlight within an hour or so of waking can help to lift mood. It will increase serotonin each day so that, along with several other daily nature-based routines and activities, will go some way to warding off SAD.

Small routines and rituals I find reassuring on difficult winter days

_____

_____

_____

Ways I can make it easier to sit outside on winter mornings (e.g. cushion kept near the door)

_____

_____

What I see when I sit outside to take in morning sunlight

_____

_____

_____

snowdrops

By early February snowdrops, also known as 'candlemas bells' or 'Maids of February', emerge from the soil. In folklore, snowdrops are symbols of hope and new life. Finding the first snowdrops of the year always gives me a dopamine-induced lift.

Alongside snowdrops, other signs of spring to look out for at this time of year are catkins, common gorse, pussy willow, alder flowers, coltsfoot, chickweed, lesser celandine, periwinkle, lungwort, sweet violet and forget-me-nots.

Snowdrops

Early spring flowers I have spotted

Shifts in my mood when I discover signs of spring

Seasonal Check-in

Encounters and moments that filled me with wonder this winter

_____

_____

Species I have observed this winter (include details, date and site)

_____

_____

Species I hope to observe in winters to come

_____

_____

_____

_____

*Ways I have lifted my mood
during winter*

Barn owl

What I am looking forward to in spring

Suppliers

If you'd like to grow some flowers from seed (see page 22) then go to www.higgledygarden.com where my friend Ben Ranyard has a gorgeous selection.

For truly beautiful stationery including pens and sketchbooks to make drawings of things you find, go to www.presentandcorrect.com or visit their gorgeous bricks and mortar shop at 12 Bury Place, London.

Acknowledgements

Thanks and love to Cindy and Rachael who have helped keep me going in the last year, thanks to my patient and brilliant agent Juliet, to Louise, Nicki and the truly wizard-like team at Michael O'Mara, to Chris Packham, who has been so kind and encouraging since the pandemic, and to all those who follow me on Twitter: this book is for you.